THIS BOOK BELONGS TO

○○○○○○○○○○○○○○○○

1

COLOR TEST

4

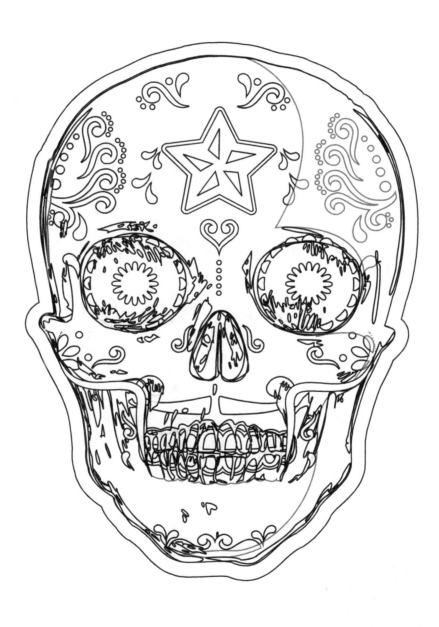

7

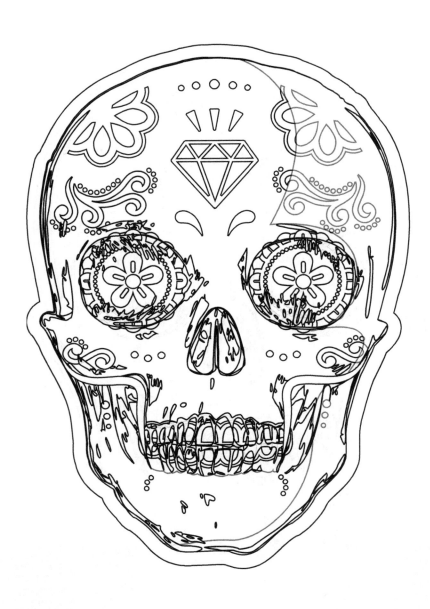

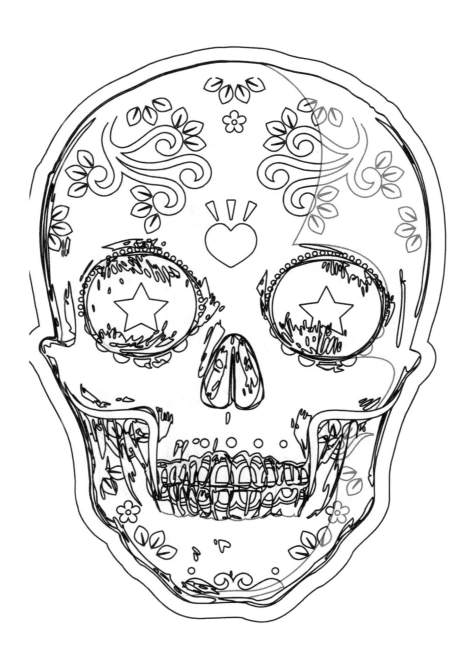

10

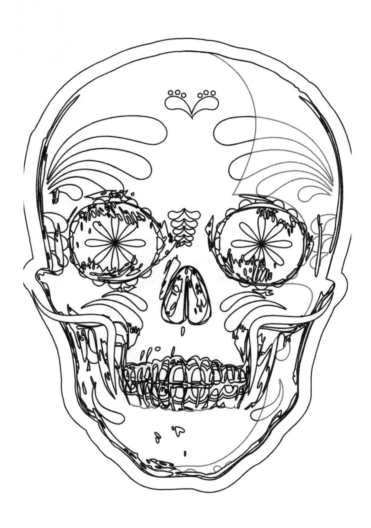

12

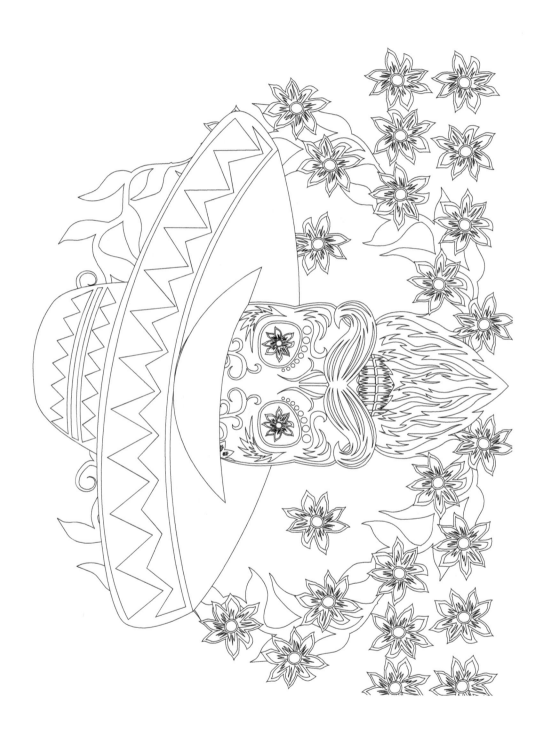

13

16

17

18

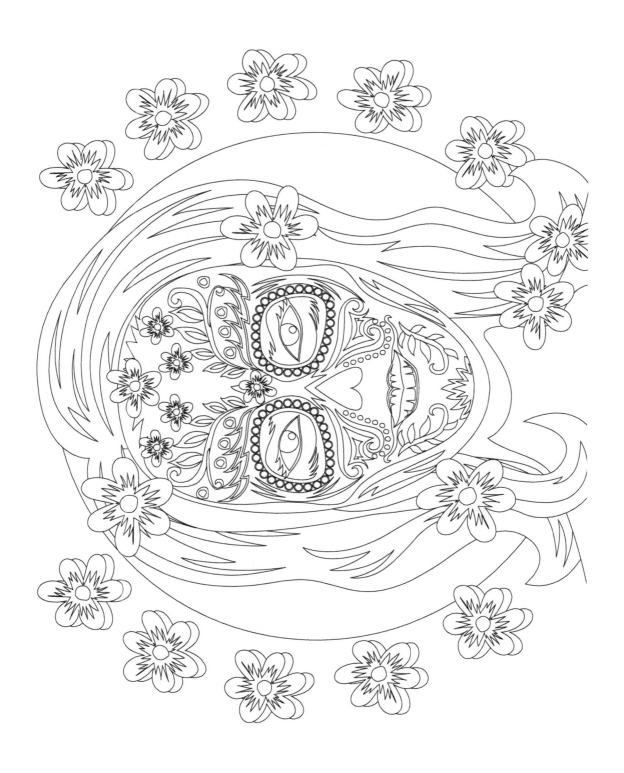

19

21

22

23

25

26

27

28

29

30

www.ingramcontent.com/pod-product-compliance
Lightning Source LLC
LaVergne TN
LVHW081625121224
798986LV00013B/1216